Micro Ran

Southwold Walks

15 Walks in and around Southwold

Geoff Gostling

ISBN 0-9525478-7-2

Printed by Portman Press
Published by G J Gostling
Copyright © G J Gostling

To the best of my knowledge, information supplied in this book
is accurate, and rights of way were correct at the time of writing.
No responsibility is accepted for acts of trespass, problems arising
from rerouting of paths, or misread instructions.

CONTENTS

Foreword 3

Introduction 4

About the Area 4

Walks

1	Dunwich Circular	(2½km, 1½m)	6
2	Westleton Heath and Dunwich Forest	(6km, 4m)	8
3	Dunwich Forest and Dunwich Beach	(7½ km, 4½m)	10
4	Westwood Marshes and Dunwich Forest	(10km, 6½m)	12
5	Newdelight Walks and Westwood Marshes	(9½km, 6m)	14
6	Walberswick, Westwood Marshes and Beach	(3km, 2m)	16
7	Walberswick Common and Westwood Marshes	(7km, 4½m)	18
8	Walberswick Common and Church	(4km, 2½m)	20
9	Wenhaston and Blackheath	(6km, 4m)	22
10	Blythburgh and Wenhaston	(7km, 4½m)	24
11	Blythburgh River Walk (East)	(5km, 3m)	26
12	Southwold Beach, Harbour and Town Marsh	(4km, 2½m)	28
13	Southwold Circular	(3½km, 2m)	30
14	Reydon, Buss Creek and Southwold Beach	(6km, 3½m)	32
15	Reydon, Southwold Beach and Covehithe	(12km, 7½m)	34

Outline Map showing start points of walks 36

Foreword

Micro Ramblers are local walk books. Each book in the series contains 15 walks in a comparatively small area. These are always circular, and often linked so that two or more may be joined to form longer walks if required.

Instructions for each individual walk are contained on the right-hand page, with the relevant map on the left, so there's no need to turn over pages while you're walking (unless you're joining 2 or more together).

The average length of walks in this book is 6km (4 miles). The map scale is 4cm to 1km or 2½in to 1 mile. (Not the map on page 36 or the Town walk)

All walks use rights of way*, permissive paths or unclassified roads. Limited use is made of main roads for joining paths or getting to and from car parks.

Distances are given in metres and kilometres. If you're more at home with yards and miles, it may be of help to remember that 1 yard is about 1 metre, 800 metres is a half-mile, 1½km is about 1 mile.

Times are based on average walking speeds. As a rough guide, at an average walking speed, it takes about 12 minutes to walk 1km, or just over 1 minute to walk 100m.

Country Walking

*Right of Way means that you have a right of passage over the ground, but no right to stray from the path. You also have a right to expect that paths be unobstructed. Clearly farmers have to work the land, but footpaths should be rolled within 2 weeks of ploughing, if weather permits.

Please remember the Country Code. Machinery, livestock and crops are the farmers livelihood. Help them, and help preserve wildlife by observing a few simple rules:

Guard against risk of fire;	Take litter home
Protect wildlife plants & trees;	Use gates & stiles to cross fences;
Fasten gates;	Leave livestock alone;
Keep pets under control;	Don't pollute water;
Keep to rights of way;	Don't make unnecessary noise;

Introduction

This book contains 15 walks within a 5 mile (8 km) radius of Southwold. It could well have been titled Sandlings Walks Part III, since it continues where Sandlings Walks Part II left off, and the variety of walks is similar, consisting of heathland, forest, small villages, river banks and seashore.

Although most of the forest walks are on public footpaths and bridleways, some of the routes use forestry tracks and rides which aren't rights of way. Forest Enterprise welcomes walkers in most parts of the forest but reserve the right to close some of the tracks without notice. If you do find a track closed, there is usually a viable parallel alternative without taking you too much out of the way.

Several of the walks involve river bank or beach walking. Normally, these should present no problem, but at some high tides they may be covered. If this is the case, take an alternative route if available, or wait for the tide to fall.

All walks are contained in Landranger Sheet 156, and you may find this useful in getting to start points. (Grid references are provided in the heading information for each walk). If you haven't got Landranger 156, the outline map on page 36 may help.

About the Area

Blythburgh: Few people travelling the A12 can fail to admire the magnificent church of the Holy Trinity, high above the surrounding marshes. In fact, the church is just one of the village's charms. For a good day out, try Walk 10, followed by some refreshment at the White Hart. After this, take a look round the church and the village, then top it off with Walk 11.

Covehithe: The amazing thing about the ruins of the old church in Covehithe is that it was ever built at all. It wasn't overtaken by some dreadful calamity - the village never had a big enough population to fill it, so it was dismantled and used to build the present St Andrew's Church. As at Dunwich, the cliffs at Covehithe have been eroded by the sea. No pub I'm afraid. (Walk 15)

Dunwich: In King John's day, this was only slightly smaller than Ipswich, with 9 churches and 2 monasteries. Most of it now lies under the sea and not one of the original churches remains. Now there are a few houses, a good museum, the Ship pub, a fish and chip restaurant, and the gateway to Greyfriars Priory. (Walks 1 and 3)

Easton Bavents   The whole coastline from Lowestoft to Aldeburgh has changed dramatically over the years. Easton Bavents may have been as much as 5 miles inland! Now the few remaining houses are in danger of toppling into the sea.

Reydon: Because you can hardly 'see the join' you could be forgiven for thinking that Reydon is a modern suburb of Southwold. However it is a village in it's own right, with an interesting church, and a pretty group of almshouses in Covert Road. (Walks 14 and 15) Pub: The Cricketers

Southwold: You almost feel that you're stepping back in time in Southwold. The feeling may be due to the haphazard grouping of buildings, interspersed by many 'greens'. There was a disastrous fire in 1659, which destroyed much of the town. As a result, the greens were left as firebreaks when the town was rebuilt. The skyline is dominated by the magnificent church of St. Edmund's, the white painted lighthouse, and, less happily, a large ugly water tower. There are lots of things to see in Southwold - too many to mention here. Try Walk 13, which takes you past several interesting features.

Walberswick: The name originates from 'Waldberts harbour'. The size of the ruins by the church of St Andrew is an indication of how wealthy the village was at one time. However this church was preceded by yet another, which stood on the marshes - this was dismantled in the 15th century and no trace remains. The current church of St Andrew is just a part of a larger church, dedicated in 1493. This was of a comparable size with the churches at Southwold and Blythburgh. In 1696 it was dismantled leaving only the Tower and the south aisle, making up the existing church. The village is popular with visitors, and probably best visited on a weekday. It supports several restaurants and pubs. Mary's Restaurant, The Potter's Wheel, and The Parish Lantern all provide good food, and so do The Anchor and the Bell Inn. (Walks 6, 7 and 8).

Wenhaston: A pleasant heathland village, west of the A12 near Blythburgh. There are 2 good pubs, The Compasses and The Star. St Peter's church was mentioned in the Domesday Book and contains a medieval painting of the Last Judgment, known as 'The Doom'. (Walk 9)

Westleton: An attractive village, with a green and a duckpond. There are plenty of good walks on the heath. There is an inn, The Crown, and a pub, the White Horse. (Walk 2 starts about 1km from the village)

Map 1

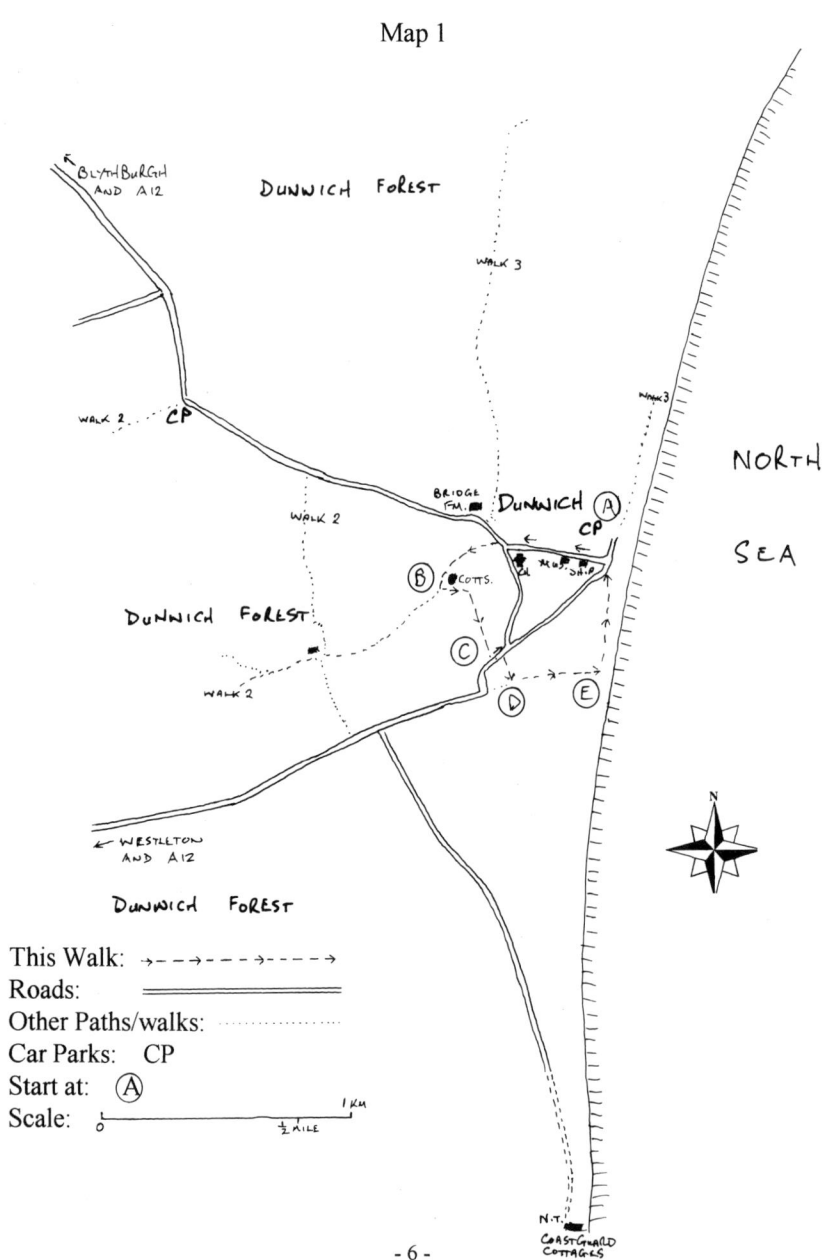

Walk 2

Distance: 6km (4 m) 1-1½ hours
Start Point: Westleton Heath (GR 454695)
Route: Westleton Heath, Dunwich Forest
Pub: None on route
Car Parking: 1km along the Dunwich road from Westleton, go straight onto the heath on a wide stony track where the road bends slightly right.

A. Stay on the wide stony track over the heath, heading for the forest. Where the track bends sharp left at the edge of the forest, go straight on along a pleasant grassy forest ride. In 700m, you'll reach an apparent choice of 3 paths. Here, go very briefly left then right again on a well trodden path in the same direction as before. In about 200m you'll pass some red brick farm buildings on the left, and then a house.

B: Just after the house, turn left on a signed path. Follow the field edge to reach the forest, then keep more or less straight on for about 1km to reach a road. Turn left on the road and walk along as far as the signed Forest Enterprise car park on the left on a right hand bend in about 600m.

C: Turn left on the signposted grassy path next to the entrance to the car park. The path soon heads gently downhill, to reach a stile in about 500m. Cross the stile and continue downhill to cross a bridge in 150m.

D: Immediately after the bridge, follow the lane left, then right along the field edge, with the hedge on your right. Keep more or less straight on along this clear path to reach another stile in about 700m.

E: After crossing the stile keep straight on. In about 150m the path merges with a wider track. Continue on this track to reach a T-junction with a wide stony forestry road in another 150m.

E: Turn briefly right on the forest road, then left again, soon heading gently downhill. At the bottom, pass between wooden posts into a sandy lane. Turn left, and stay in the lane to reach the road in about 500m.

F: Turn left on the road to return to Westleton Heath in about 500m.

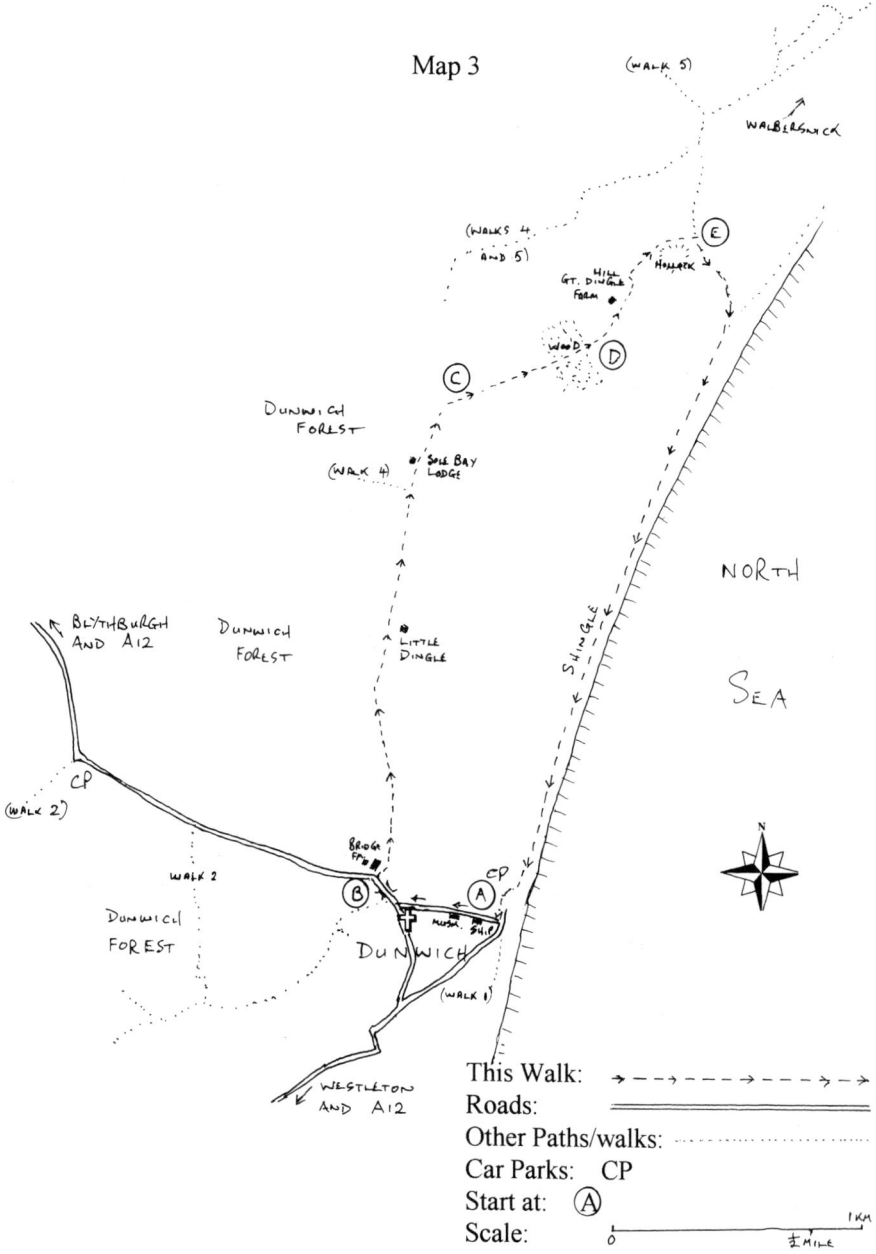

Walk 3

Distance: 7½km (4½ m) 1½-2 hours
Start Point: Beach Car Park, Dunwich (GR 479708)
Route: Dunwich Forest, Dunwich Beach
Pub: Ship Inn, Dunwich
Car Parking: As above
Going: Mostly easy, but can be fairly hard work on the beach

A: Go back along the road, and walk up past the Ship Inn and the Dunwich Museum. Just after passing the church follow the road round to the right. Shortly after crossing the bridge you'll reach a signed bridleway on the right.

B: Turn right on the bridleway, keeping to the right of farm buildings. Stay on the main track for about 2km, following frequent signs for the 'Suffolk Coast and Heaths Path'. 300m after passing 'Sole Bay Lodge', a white weatherboarded bungalow, the track bends right, away from the edge of the forest and becomes a hedged lane.

C: Follow the hedged lane slightly downhill - you should get some good views of Westwood Marshes over to the left. At the bottom of the lane pass through the gate and continue through the small wood.

D: On the other side of the wood, follow the Suffolk Coast and Heaths Path signs, taking you round to the right of Great Dingle Hill. (Altitude 5m!) Follow the clear path round to the other side of the hill to reach a path on a low bank. Turn right on the path, which will take you round the rear of a small hillock. Shortly after rounding the hillock, you'll reach a signed T-junction with a well used path.

E: Turn right on the path and follow it to reach the shore in about 400m. Turn right on the shore to reach Dunwich in about 2½km.

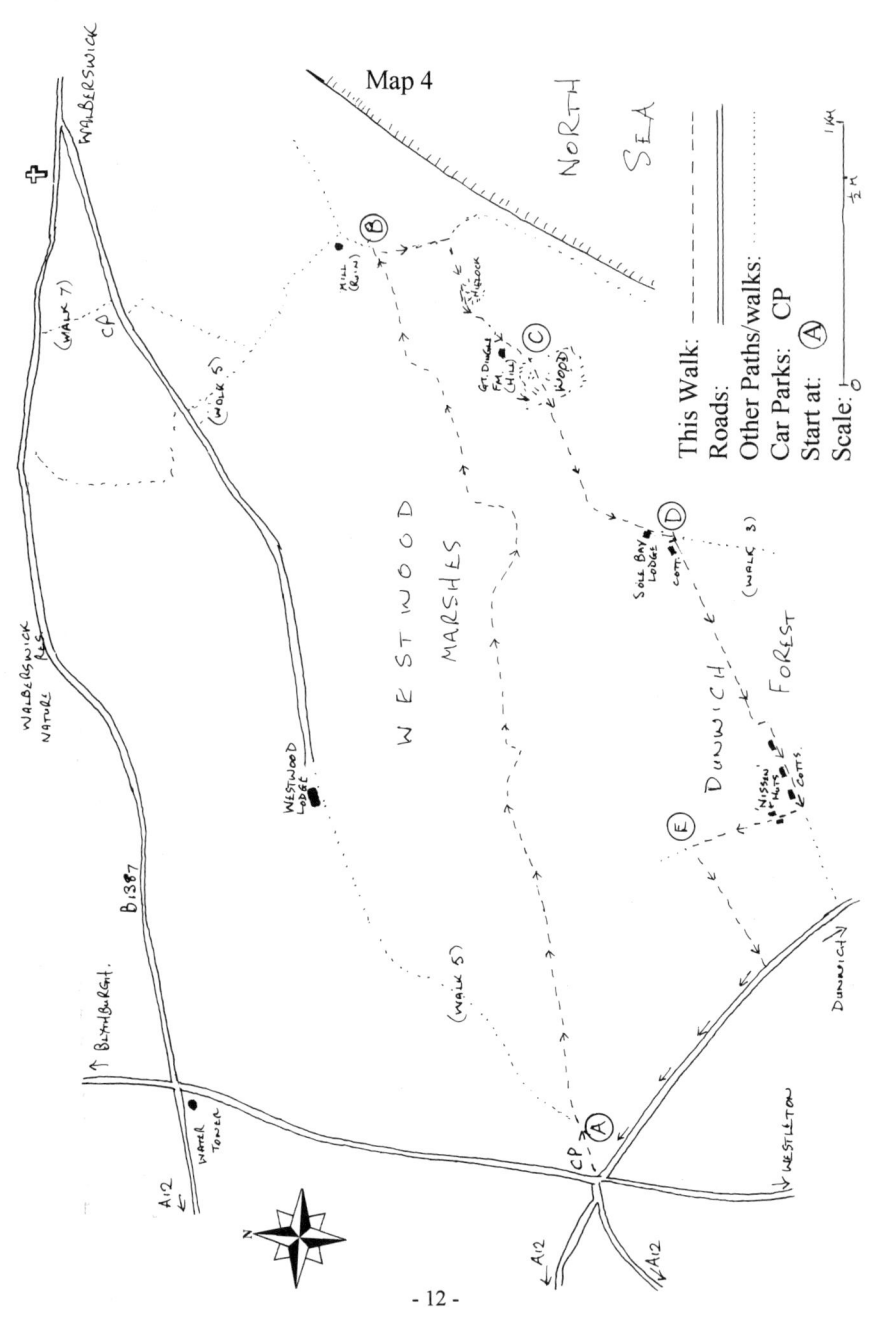

Walk 4

Distance: 10km (6½ m) 2 - 3 hours
Start Point: Small Car Park, Blythburgh-Westleton Road (GR 451726)
Route: Westwood Marshes and Dunwich Forest
Pub: None on route (2 in Walberswick)
Car Parking: Unofficial Car park on 5-way junction 3km (2m) south of Blythburgh on Blythburgh - Westleton road (B1125).
Going: Muddy in places - stout shoes or boots are recommended..

*N.B. Forest rides in **D** and **E** below are not rights of way, but walkers are welcomed at Forest Enterprise discretion. Also, please be aware that some of the rides are Permit Horse Trails or bike trails, and exercise due caution.*

A: Go down the broad track from the back of the car park. In about 100m, where the main track bends left, keep straight on along a signed grassy path along the fence. After entering woods, keep straight on along the clear path to reach Westwood Marshes in 1½ km. Stay on the raised bank through the marshes for another 3½km almost as far as a ruined drainage windmill.

B: About 50m before the mill, turn right on a signed path. Walk along with the river on your left for 350m, then turn right on a path following a Suffolk Coast and Heath sign. Follow the track round the back of a small hillock and on towards another small hill. Follow the sign taking you left of this 2nd hill to pass a cottage (Great Dingle Farm). Soon after the cottage, the path joins a track taking you into a small wood.

C: Follow the track through the wood, then gently uphill on a pleasant hedged lane for about 500m to reach Dunwich Forest. Stay on the track to pass a white wooden bungalow (Sole Bay Lodge) on the right. Shortly after passing the bungalow you'll reach a forest road on the right.

D: Turn right on the forest road, immediately passing a red-brick cottage. Stay on the road, following it left and right in 800m. About 350m after the bends, just after a red-brick cottage with tall square chimneys, turn right on a forestry road. After passing the first Nissen hut, continue straight on along the left hand side of the second, to head gently uphill on a grassy track. About 150m after the top of the hill, you'll reach a forest ride to the left.

E: Turn left on the ride, and keep straight on to reach a road in 500m. Turn right on the road and follow it with care for 1km to reach the car park.

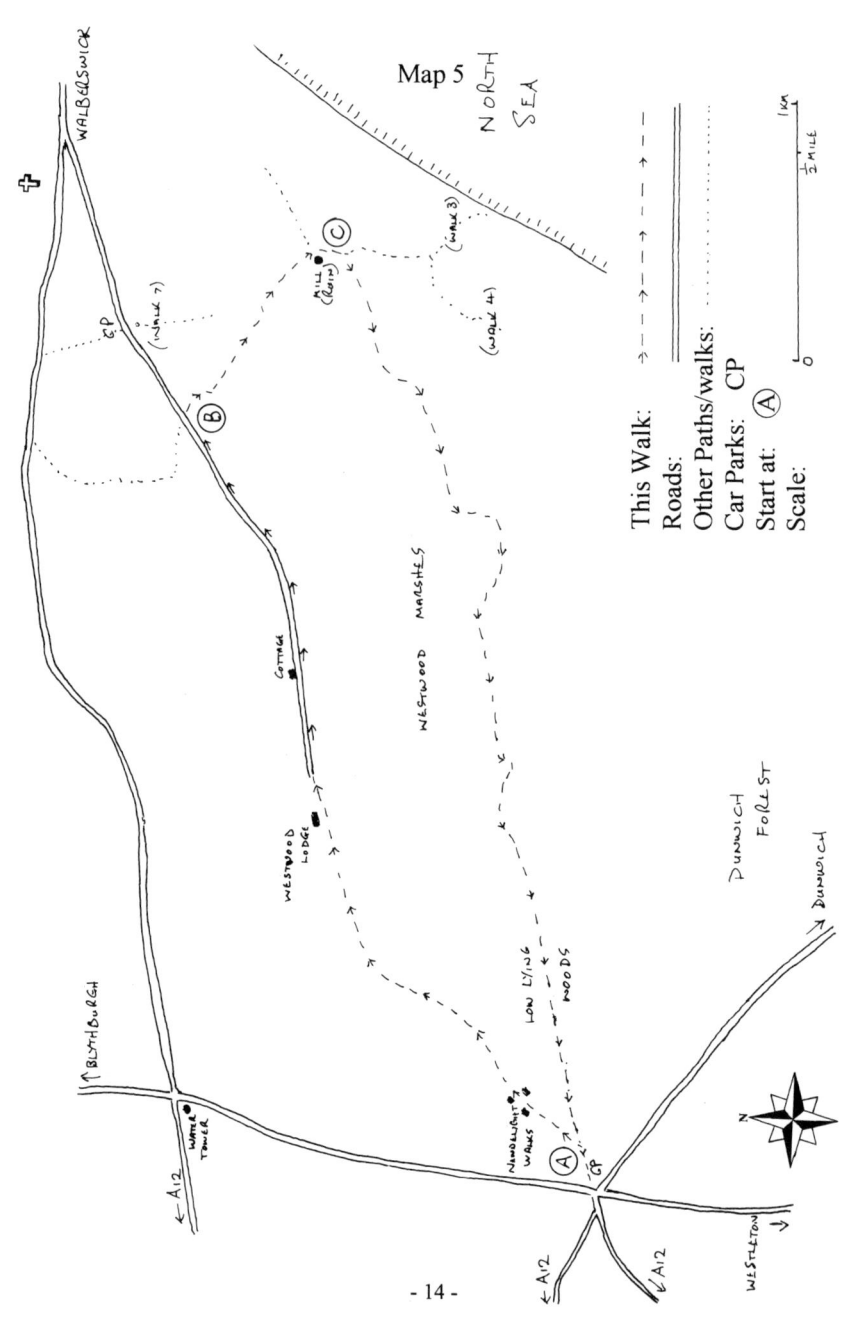

Walk 5

Distance: 9½km (6 m) 2 - 2½hours
Start Point: Blythburgh-Westleton Road (GR 451726)
Route: Newdelight Walks and Westwood Marshes
Pubs: None on route, but 2 in Walberswick and Westleton
Car Parking: Unofficial Car park on 5-way junction 3km (2m) south of Blythburgh on Blythburgh - Westleton road.
Going: FP through the marsh is slippery after wet weather.

A: Continue down the wide sandy track from the car park. In about 100m stay on it as it bends to the left. Continue on the main track to pass cottages at Newdelight Walks in about 300m, and Westwood Lodge in a further 1½km. Just after Westwood Lodge, the track becomes a metalled lane. Stay on this little used road for another 1½km (roughly 20mins walk) to reach signed footpaths to right and left.

B: Turn right on the signed path, and after a short distance take the right signed fork towards a farm gate. Just before the gate (marked 'No Entry'), turn left along a good path to reach Walberswick Nature Reserve on Westwood Marshes. Continue straight on past the ruined drainage windmill for about 50m to reach a 2-way footpath sign.

C: At the fork take the signed path to the right. The path meanders through the marsh for about 3km, its twisting route marked with occasional clumps of blackthorn, elder and rambler rose. Eventually the path enters a low lying wood. Follow the clear path through the wood, occasionally on raised boards, to reach the car park in about 1½km.

Map 6

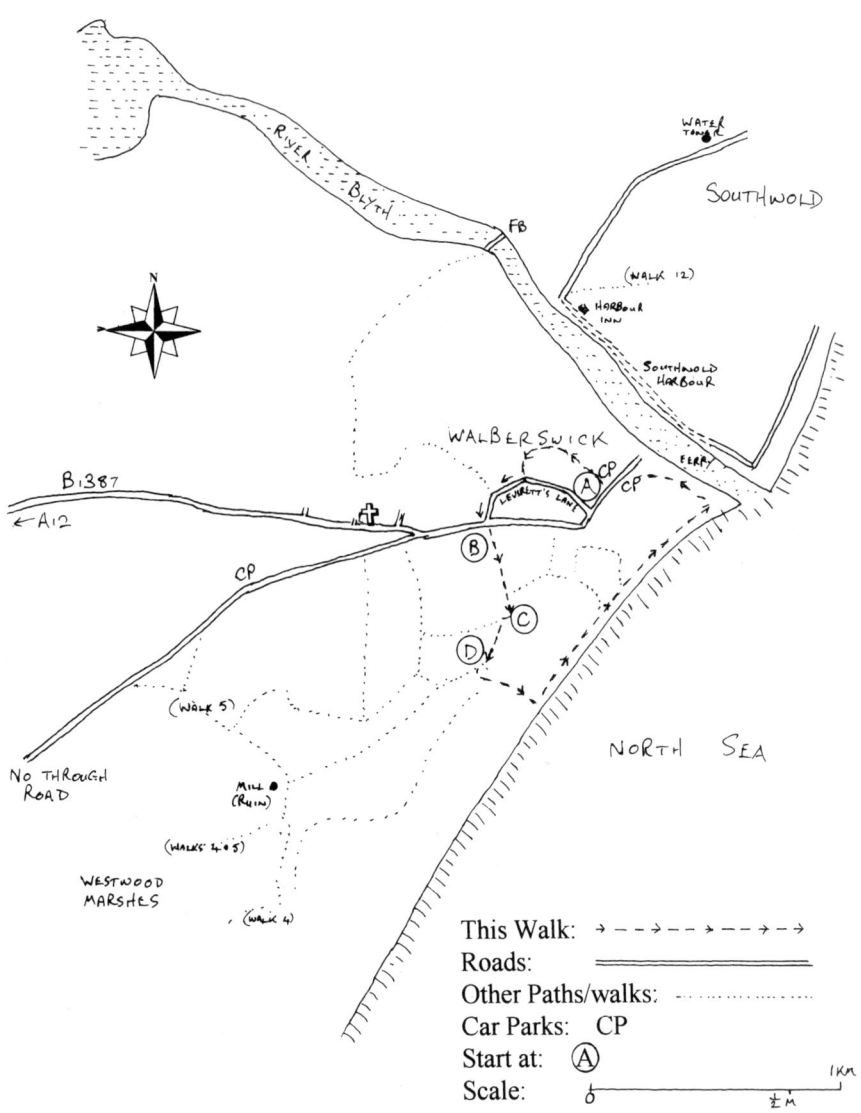

Walk 6

Distance: 3km (2 m) 1 hour approx
Start Point: Beach Car Park, Walberswick (GR 500749)
Route: Walberswick, Westwood Marshes, and the beach
Pub: The Bell Inn
Car Parking: Long narrow car park, on left near river
Going: Fairly easy

A: Go to the back of the long narrow car park at the end nearest the village. Go down the bank and cross the stile into the low lying meadow. Keep straight on to join a reedy ditch along the left side of the field and follow it for about 200m to reach a stile into a lane. Cross the stile and turn left up the lane to reach the road (Leverett's Lane). Turn right in Leverett's Lane and follow it to reach the main road in about 300m.

B: When you reach the main road, go down the signed footpath opposite. Follow this to reach Westwood Marshes, keeping close to the field edge all the way down to the bottom of the field.

C: At the bottom follow the field edge round to the right for about 50m, to find a path through the bushes onto the marsh. Follow the boarded walkway through reeds for about 250m to reach the river bank.

D: Turn right on the river bank as far as the footbridge, and cross the river. Follow the clear path to reach the beach in about 300m. Turn left on the beach and walk along almost as far as the River Blyth, before crossing the dunes to reach the car parks.

Map 7

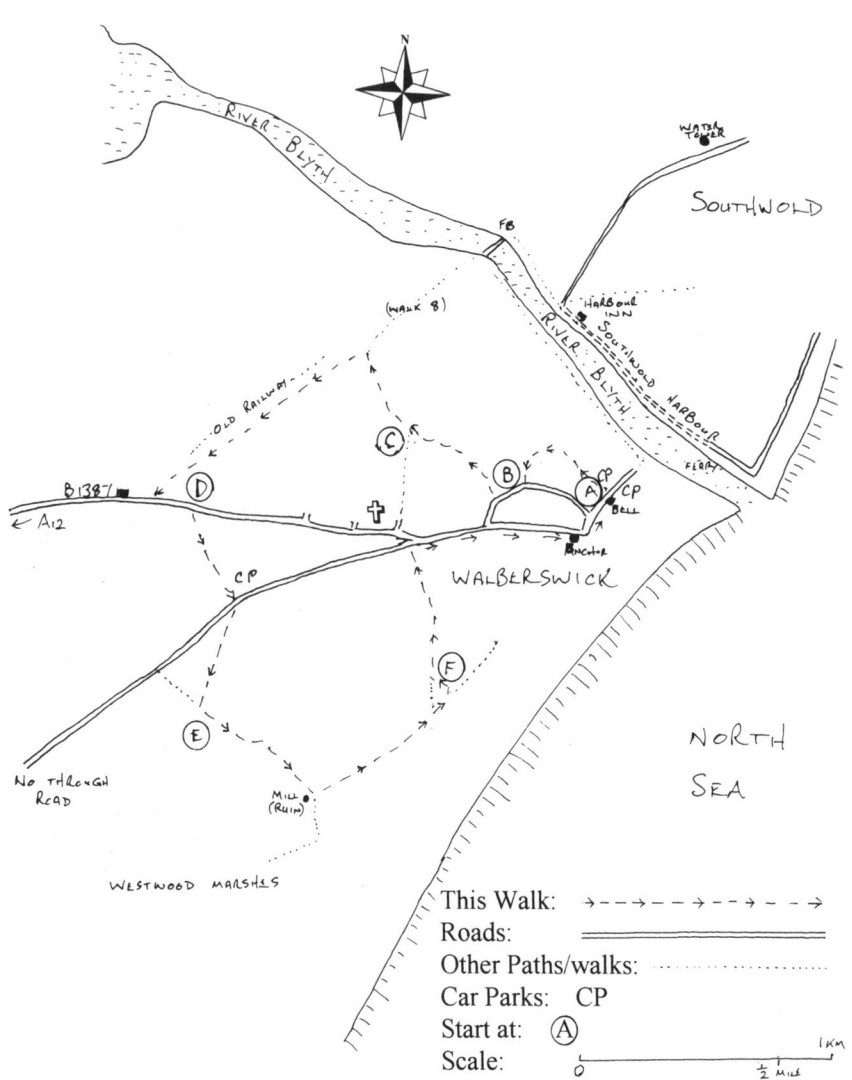

Walk 7

Distance: 7km (4½ m) 1½-2 hours
Start Point: Beach Car Park, Walberswick (GR 500749)
Route: Walberswick Common and Westwood Marshes
Pub: The Anchor and the Bell Inn
Car Parking: Long narrow car park on left near river
Going: Fairly easy

A: Leave the rear of the car park at the end nearest the village. Go down the bank and cross a stile into a low lying meadow. Keep straight ahead to join a reedy ditch and follow it for about 250m to reach a stile into a lane. Turn left up the lane and follow it uphill to reach a road (Leverett's Lane).

B: Turn right on the road for 150m to reach a left hand bend. Here turn sharp right on a path and stay on it for about 400m, ignoring various side turnings, to reach a metalled lane near the back of some red brick cottages.

C: Turn right on the metalled lane to reach the Common. Keep on for about 500m to reach a 'B.R.' (Bridleway) sign to the left, just before a small turning area on the right. Turn left on the signed bridleway, and keep more or less straight on to reach a Nature Reserve in about 500m. Go straight on through the Nature Reserve, to reach a road in about 500m.

D: Turn left on the road for 200m, then turn right across a field on a signed bridleway. (If the path isn't clear, follow the direction of the sign). On the other side of the field you'll enter a car park. Go out onto the road, and down the path almost opposite. Follow this pleasant lane, soon heading downhill, to reach a wider path at a T-junction in 500m.

E: Turn left at the junction and follow the path onto the marsh. Continue on a raised bank as far as a ruined drainage windmill, then turn left over a stile and bridge along the river bank. Stay by the river for about 800m to reach a T-junction with a grassy path by a dense patch of blackthorn.

F: Turn left at the T-junction,. The path soon bends to the right, taking you uphill along a narrow lane to reach the village. Turn right on the road and follow the village street to return to the car park, or use Leverett's Lane as an alternative if you wish.

Map 8

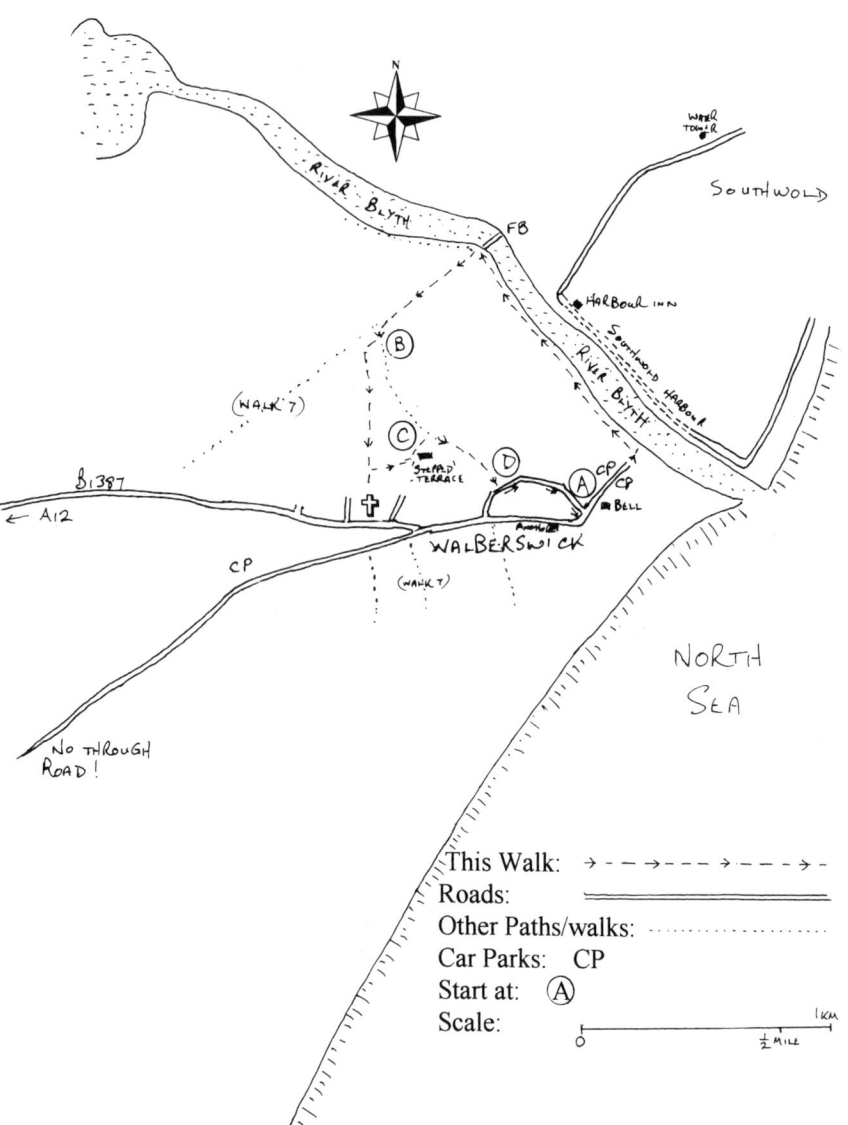

Walk 8

Distance:	4km (2½ m) 1 hour approx
Start Point:	Beach Car Park, Walberswick (GR 500749)
Route:	River wall, Walberswick Common and church
Pub:	The Bell Inn
Car Parking:	See above
Going:	Easy

A: Continue down the road to reach the river. Turn left along the river bank. When you reach the footbridge over the river in about 1km, turn left on the metalled lane. In about 600m you'll reach a small car park or turning space on the left hand side, and shortly after this you'll find a signed bridleway (signed B.R.) to the right.

B: Turn right on the signed bridleway and in about 150m turn left on a narrow path between gorse bushes, heading more or less straight for the church. In about 500m, just before reaching a metalled road, turn left on a grassy path. (If you want to visit the church, go straight up the road, then come back to this point). The grassy path soon becomes a well worn unsurfaced road. Follow this to reach a metalled lane in about 250m by an interesting 'stepped' terrace of 4 red-bricked cottages.

C: Turn left briefly on the metalled lane, then go <u>half</u> right on a grassy path. In 50m, turn right on a narrow but well-trodden footpath. Stay on this to emerge on a bend in Leverett's Lane in about 400m.

D: Turn left in Leverett's Lane and follow it to reach the village green.

Map 9

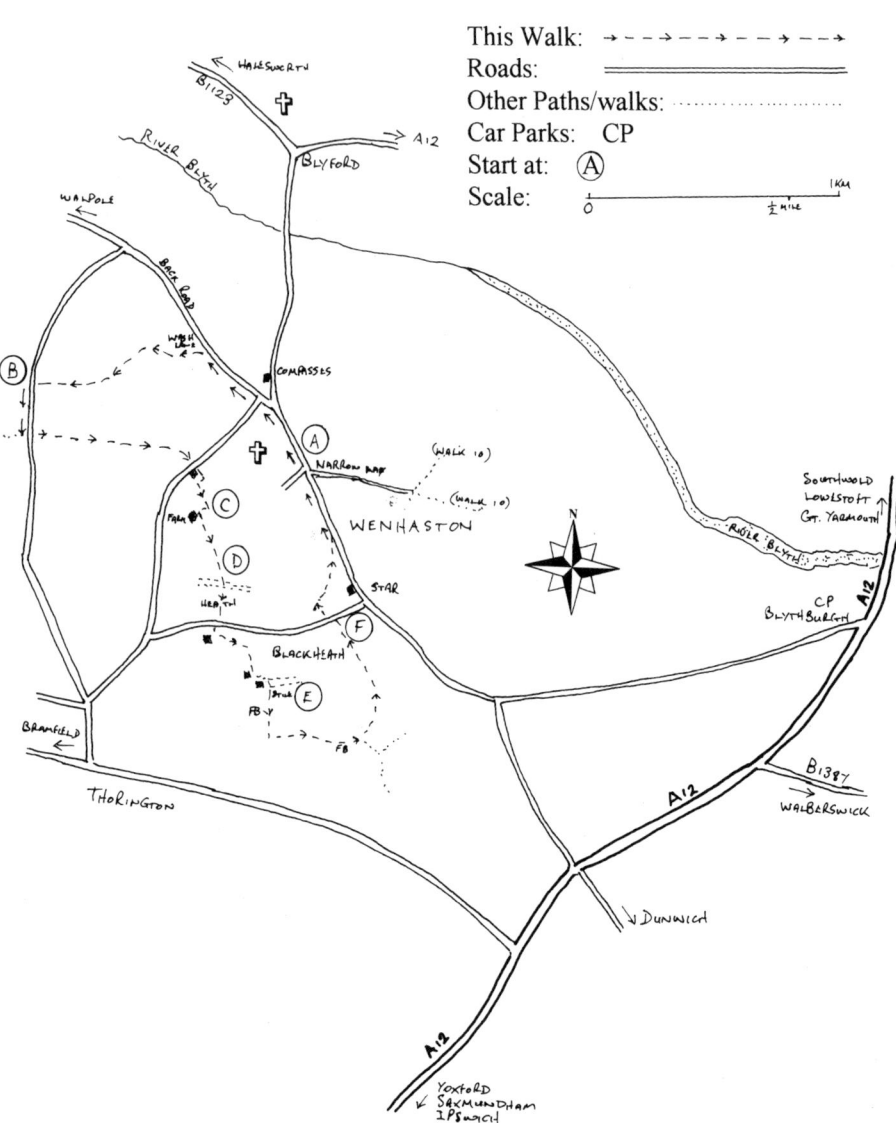

Walk 9

Distance: 6km (4 m) 1½ hours approx.
Start Point: Wenhaston Church (GR 425755)
Route: Wenhaston and Blackheath
Pub: The Star and The Compasses
Car Parking: Roadside parking near Wenhaston church
Going: Easy

A. Walk up the main road towards the Compasses. Just before the pub, turn left into Back Road. Stay on this for about 500m to reach Wash Lane on the left. Turn into Wash Lane. In 150m bear right on a shady path, to reach a field edge path. Keep on with the field edge on your right to reach a road in 600m.

B: Turn left on the road for 200m, to reach signed paths to left and right. Turn left and stay on the field edge path for 800m to reach a road opposite a white cottage. Go down the signed path left of the cottage, and at the end of the back garden, climb a stile on the right and cross a narrow field. Cross a 2nd stile and turn left alongside the hedge to reach a 3rd stile at the bottom of the field.

C: Cross this stile onto a wide field edge track. Turn right for about 50m, then, just before the farmhouse, turn left along the field edge. At the corner of the field in about 150m go through the gap, then keep on in the same direction as before across the open field along power lines to reach a lane.

D. At the lane turn briefly left then right again soon heading across the heath on roughly the same line as before, to reach a road in about 250m. At the road, go half left into the signed sandy lane opposite. Follow this for 350m, to pass 2 cottages on the right. Immediately after the second cottage (The Dell), you'll see a stile and signed footpath on the right.

E: Cross the stile and follow the path alongside the ditch, then over a small footbridge, to reach the bottom of the field in about 250m. Here turn left on a signed path for 400m, to reach a double footpath sign. Take the path to the left alongside the ditch. This soon bends left to take you up to a gate and stile leading into a lane by buildings at Blackheath. Follow the lane up to the road. *(The Star is about 200m to your right along the road)*

F: At the road go left for a short distance then turn right on a sandy track. Bear right in about 50m, soon heading uphill on a narrow gorsy path. At the 5-way junction in about 100m, take the 2nd left to continue slightly uphill and reach the road in about 150m. Continue up the road for about 500m to reach the church.

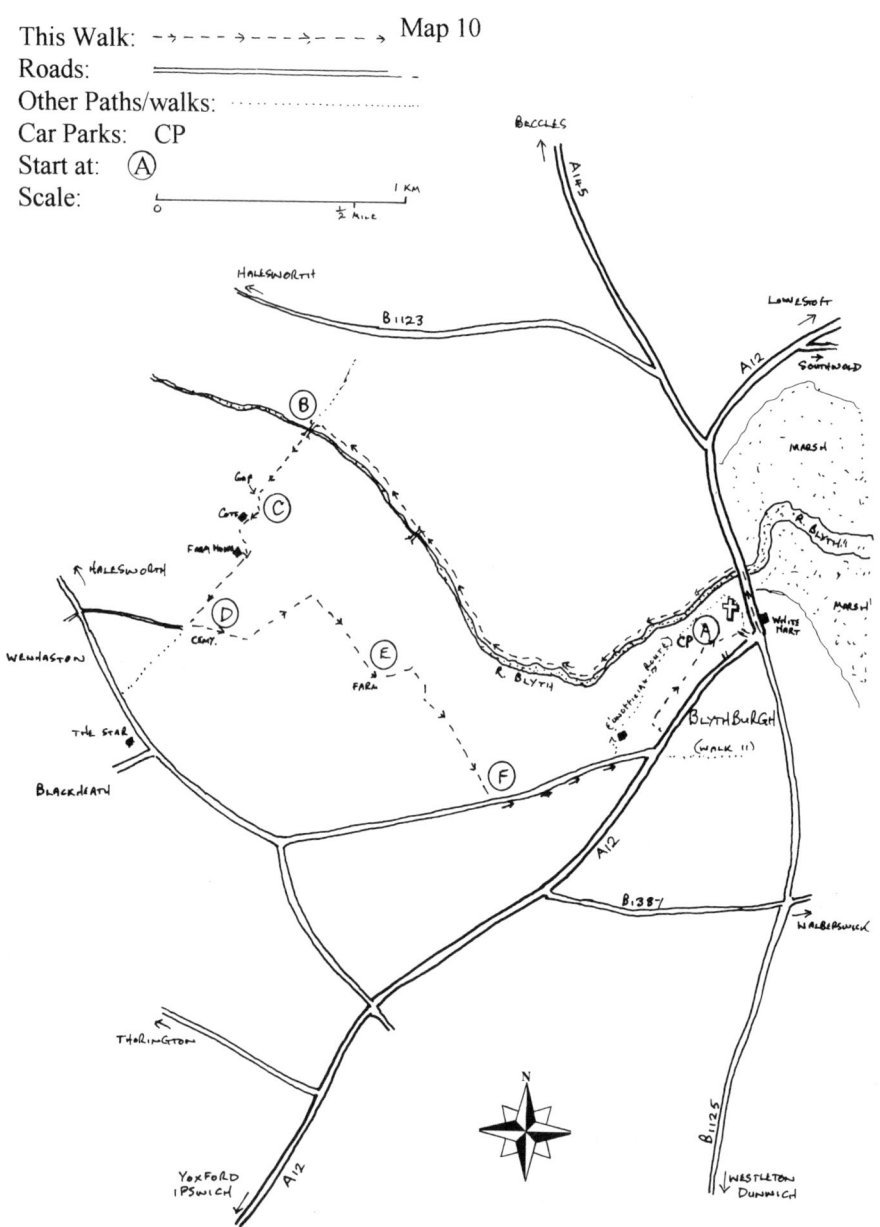

Walk 10

Distance:	7km (4½ m) 1½-2 hours
Start Point:	Blythburgh Church (GR 451754)
Route:	River bank and Wenhaston
Pub:	White Hart, Blythburgh
Car Parking:	Blythburgh church car park
Going:	The river bank is often overgrown with nettles and thistles.

A. Go down to the main road and turn left. Cross the bridge over the river, and turn left along the river bank. In 2km you'll reach a sandy field. Turn left along the fence to get on to the river bank again. Stay by the river to reach a railed bridge in 1200m. (*__Not__ the first bridge, but the second*).

B: Turn left over the railed bridge to cross the river and follow waymarks to cross 2 small footbridges. About 50m after crossing the 2nd, go through a gap on the left into the next field and head for the stile and gate in the corner

C: Cross the stile and continue on the track on the other side. The track takes you past a cottage then a farm, and then bends right slightly uphill towards Wenhaston. At the top of the hill you'll reach a metalled road with bungalows to the right, a FP sign straight ahead and another to the left.

D: Turn sharp left on the signed path along a lane, passing a cemetery. Continue along the lane as it bends to the left downhill, and then to the right at the bottom. About 400m after the right turn you'll reach a farm.

E: Where the road bends right between farm buildings, go straight on through a gate, and follow the track to reach a gate/ stile onto a grassy track. Follow this as it swings right in 150m soon crossing a bridge to reach a stile. Cross the stile and go half left to another stile in about 50m. After crossing this go very slightly right to another stile in the fence on the other side of the field, and then onward to a gap onto a road. (Wenhaston Lane).

F: Turn left on Wenhaston Lane. *150m before the A12, you'll see a short road on the left, leading to a small building. Behind this is a well maintained, frequently walked path, leading directly to the back of the church. However, it isn't an 'official' right of way.* The far less pleasant 'official' route is to walk along to the A12, cross with care, turn left for 100m, then cross again onto a signed path on the left, which soon leads onto a field edge, then into a lane to take you back to the church.

Map 11

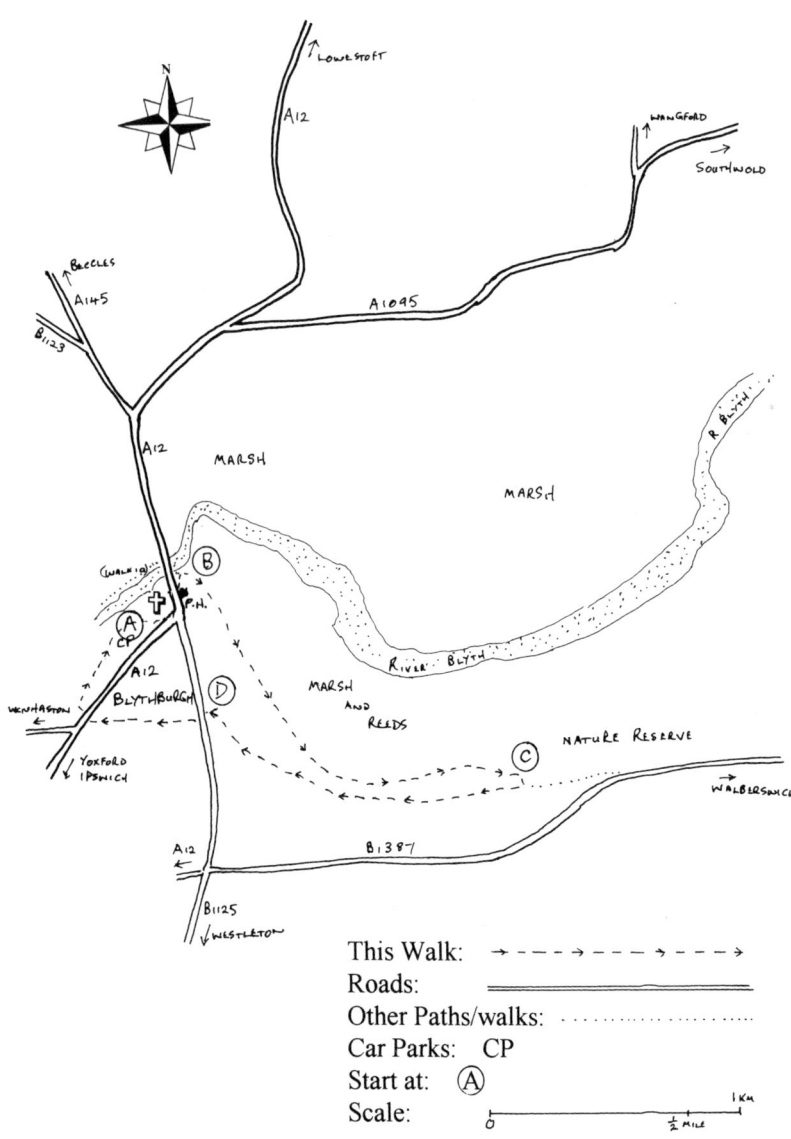

Walk 11

Distance: 5km (3 m) 1-1½ hours
Start Point: Blythburgh Church car park (GR 451754)
Route: The Blyth River, east of Blythburgh
Pub: White Hart, Blythburgh
Car Parking: Blythburgh church car park
Going: Easy.

A: Go out onto the road and follow it round to reach the A12. Cross the main road with care and turn left down to the White Hart. Take the unsurfaced lane running from the front of the pub towards the river.

B: About 50m along the lane turn right through a narrow gap, soon passing through a kissing gate onto the river bank. Follow this pleasant path along the embankment, soon through reeds, then woodland for about 2km, to reach an official sign informing you that you can go no further unless riding a horse (!!).

C: Turn right on the signed footpath to reach another good path in about 50m. Turn right on this track and follow it for about 1½km to reach a road.

D: At the road go slightly left to find another footpath almost opposite. Follow this for about 500m to reach the main A12. Turn right for a few steps, then cross with great care onto the signed path opposite. The short lane soon enters a field. Follow the field edge for about 150m to enter the end of a lane via a stile, and continue on towards the church. In about 200m look for a gap on the right into the church car park.

Map 12

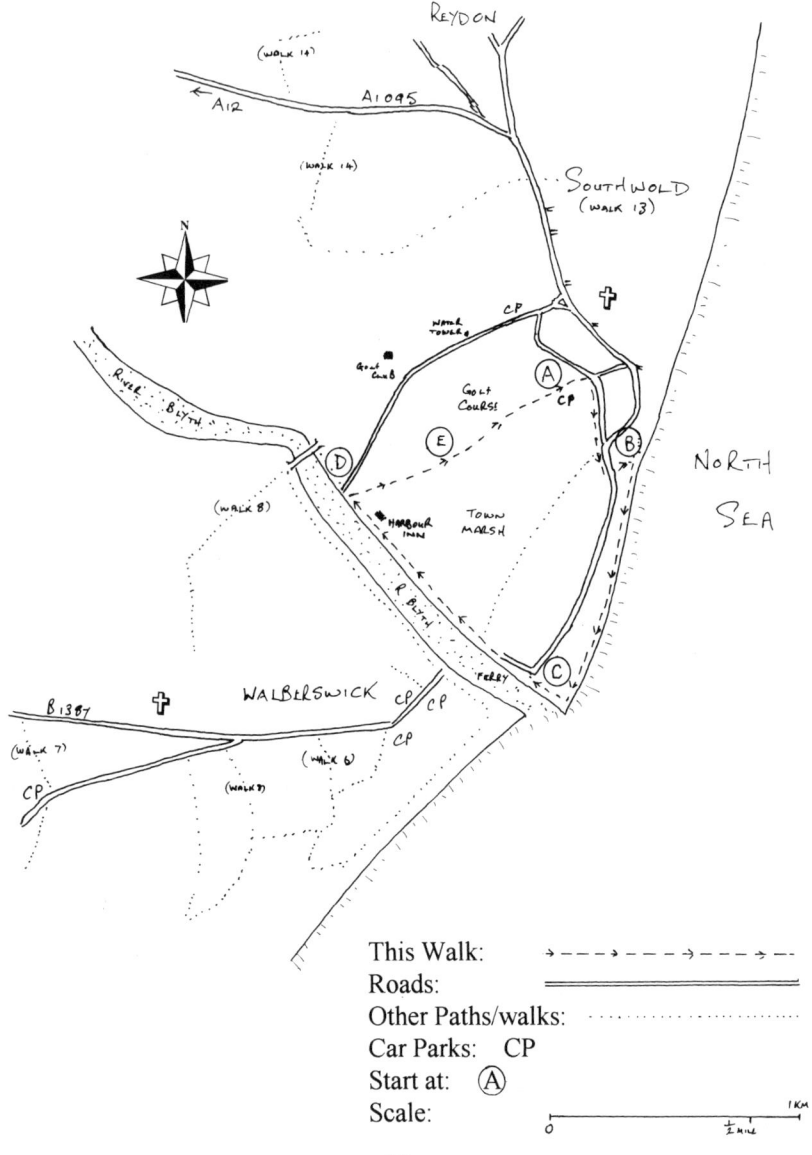

- 28 -

Walk 12

Distance: 4km (2½ m) 1-1½ hours
Start Point: Junction of Godyll Rd and Gardner Rd (GR 507760)
Route: Southwold beach, Southwold Harbour, Town Marshes
Pub: Harbour Inn
Car Parking: Free at the junction of Godyll Road and Gardner Road

A: Leave the car park, and turn right down Gardner Road, (signposted 'the Harbour') to reach Ferry Road in 250m. Carry straight on along Ferry Road for 150m, then turn left on a path uphill to reach Gun Hill.

B: Go down onto the beach and turn right. Stay on the beach for about 1½km to reach the entrance to the River Blyth.

C: Turn right along the river to reach the Harbour Inn in about 1km.

D: Very shortly after passing the Harbour Inn, turn right on a narrow road, and in a few steps turn right through a gateway onto a signed path.

E: Follow the path across the Town Marshes to reach the car park, crossing four footbridges on the way.

Map 13

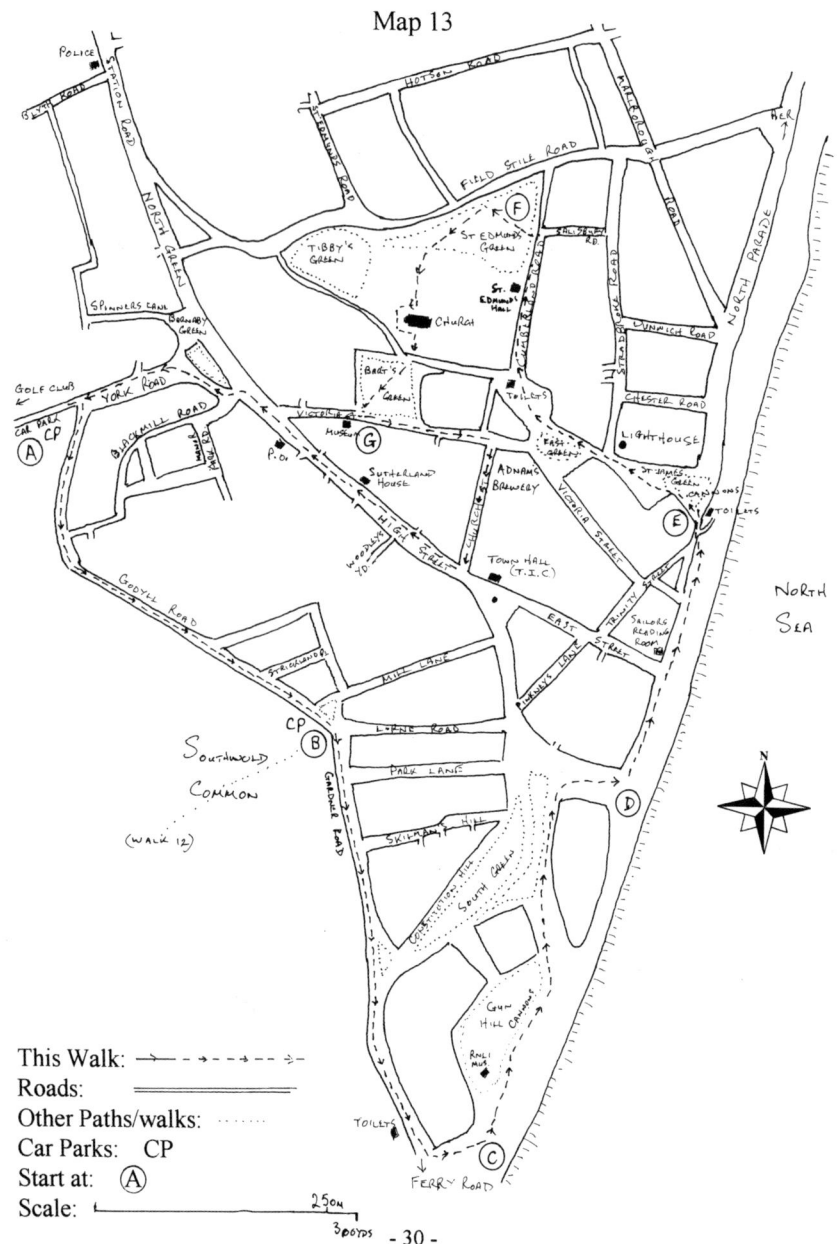

Walk 13

Distance: 3½km (2 m) 1-1½ hours
Start Point: Golf Club Road (Access via York Road) (GR 504764)
Route: Southwold circular walk
Pub: Various
Car Parking: Free parking on road leading to Golf Club. See above

A: Go back up the road towards the town. Before reaching York Road, turn right on Godyll Road. Continue down Godyll Road, along the edge of the Common to reach the junction with Gardner Road.

B: Turn right down Gardner Road, (signposted 'the Harbour') to reach Ferry Road in 250m. Carry straight on along Ferry Road for 150m, then turn left on a path uphill to reach Gun Hill.

C: Stay on the upper promenade to pass the *Lifeboat Museum* and cannons on *Gun Hill*, then bear left, to reach South Green. Keep to the right at South Green, then turn right back to the promenade.

D: Turn left on the promenade to pass the *Sailors Reading Room* and reach St James Green with 2 cannons and a flagpole in a further 200m.

E: Turn into St. James Green, with *the Lighthouse* in Stradbrooke Road on your right and *Adnam's Brewery* on your left. Keep straight on through East Green to reach Cumberland Road on the right. Turn right into Cumberland Road, soon passing a school and then St Edmund's Hall on the left. 50m after this, you'll reach a path on the left across St Edmund's Green.

F: Take the path across St Edmund's Green. Don't go out onto the road on the other side but follow the path into the churchyard. Go through to the front of *St Edmund's Church*. From the gates at the front cross the road and go diagonally right across Bartholomew's Green to reach *the Museum*.

G: At the museum, turn left on Victoria Street for about 150m then turn right into Church Street. Note the attractively painted cottages on the right. At the end of Church Street, you'll reach High Street, with the *Market Place* to your left. Turn right in High Street, and walk along for about 300m, passing *Sutherland House* on your right, before reaching York Road on your left.

Map 14

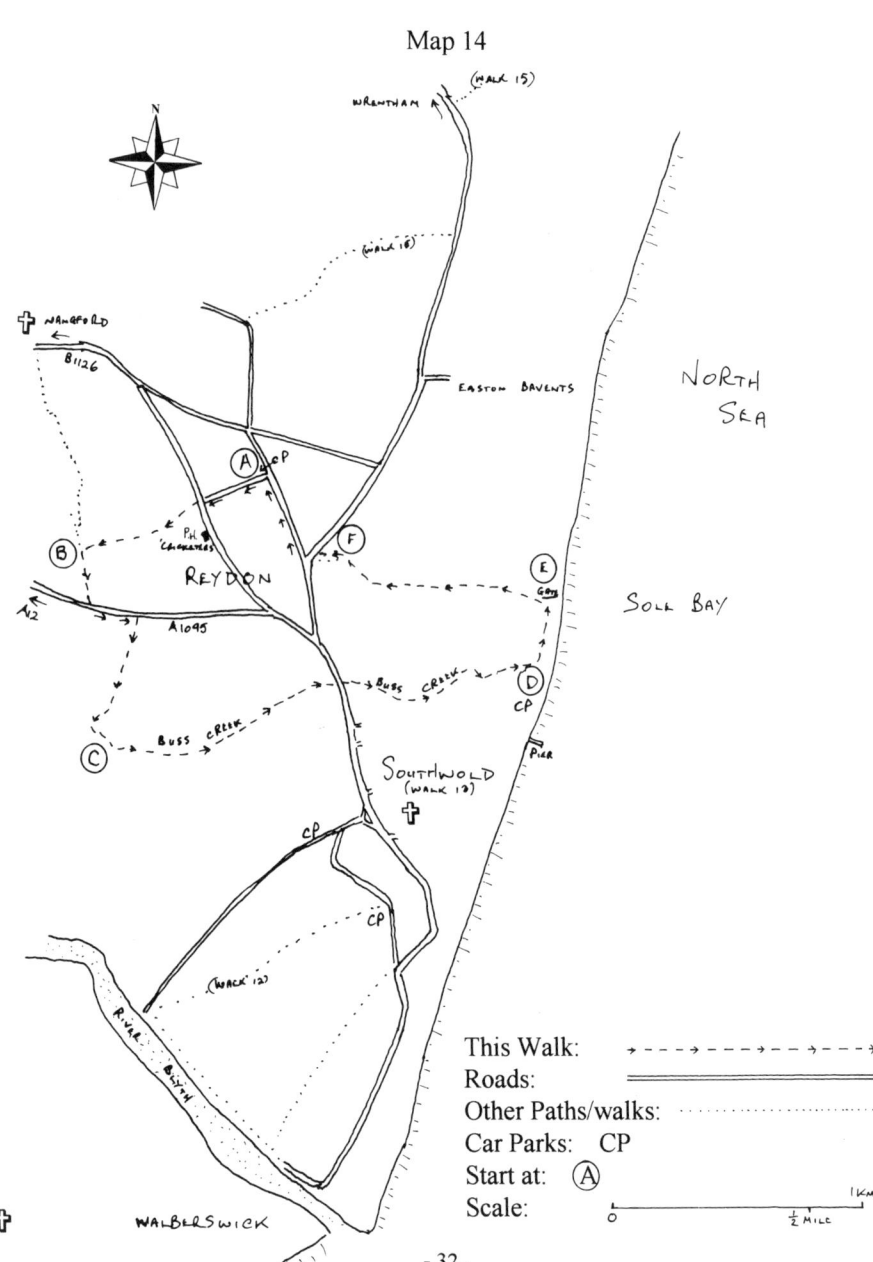

Walk 14

Distance: 6km (3½ m) 1½ hours approx
Start Point: Reydon (GR 501777)
Route: Reydon, Buss Creek, Southwold Beach
Pub: The Cricketers, Reydon
Car Parking: Junction of Covert Road and Jermyns Road

To reach the car park from Southwold, leave the town via the main road. About 200m after passing over Mights Bridge (crossing Buss Creek) turn right on the Lowestoft Road. In about 300m, take the left fork into Covert Road, and continue for about 400m to reach the free car park on the corner of Jermyns Road.

A: Turn right out of the car park and walk up Jermyns Road. When you reach the main road in about 300m, go straight ahead on Keens Lane. (*The Cricketers is about 100m to the left down the main road*) In about 500m you'll pass Laurel Farm on the right.

B: At the T-junction, just after passing Laurel Farm, turn left and walk along to the main road. Turn left on the main road for 200m then turn right on a narrow path. In about 400m, almost opposite a gate on the left into the Angling Club grounds, turn right. In about 100m, you'll reach a junction. Turn left at the junction, and follow the path to reach a 4-way footpath sign in about 150m.

C: Turn left at the 4-way sign and follow the bank, with Buss Creek on your left, to reach the main road in about 1km. Cross the road and go straight on through trees on the other side, still following the creek. In about 1km you'll reach Southwold beach car park, with the pier over to your right.

D: Turn left in the beach car park, go through the gateway on the permissive path, and follow it along for about 200m to a farm gate marked 'Private'.

E: At the gate, turn left on a path signed 'Suffolk Coast and Heaths path'. Follow this for about 1km to reach the Lowestoft Road.

F: At the Lowestoft Road, turn briefly left then right into Covert Road. Jermyns Road is on the left in about 400m.

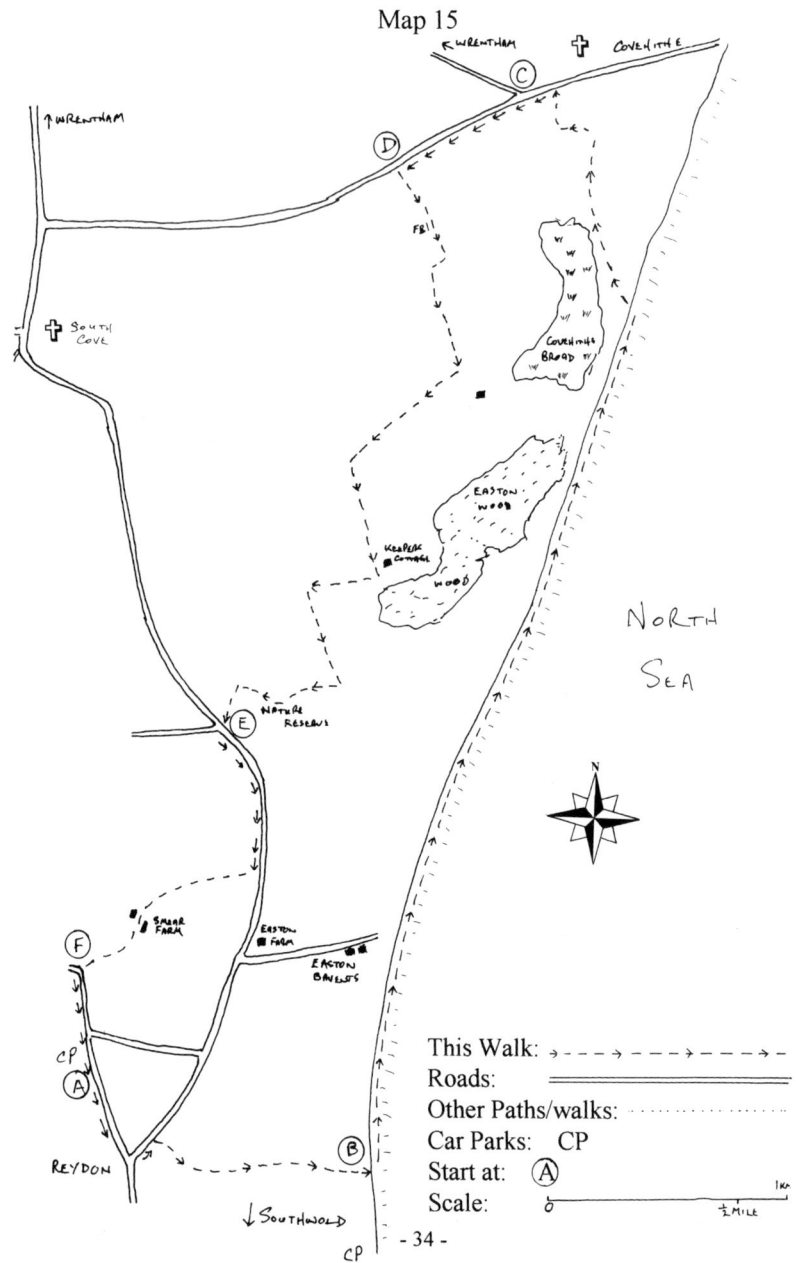

Walk 15

Distance: 12km (7½ m) 3-4 hours.
Start Point: Reydon (GR 501777)
Route: Reydon, Southwold Beach, Covehithe
Pub: None on route
Car Parking: As for Walk 14
Going: Heavy on the beach and wet in the nature reserve (Para D).

The beach section from Southwold towards Covehithe (Section B) is covered at high tide. Consult tide tables, and do it on a falling tide.

A: Leave the car park and walk along Covert Road towards Southwold. When you reach a major road (Lowestoft Road) in 400m, turn left, and cross to the signed footpath opposite. Follow it for 1km to reach the beach.

B: Turn left on the beach. (*See above note*) 3km (about 2m) distant you may be able to see woods next to the beach. After passing the woods, the cliffs drop to beach level and you'll pass Covehithe Broad. Just after this, where the cliffs start to rise from the shore again, take a path through bracken, parallel with the shore at first, but soon turning away. Stay on the signed path to reach the road near the church in Covehithe.

C: At the road, turn left, keeping left at the fork. Stay on the road for 700m, to reach a signed path to the left.

D: Turn left and follow Suffolk Heath and Coast Path signs. After several signed right and left turns, in about 2½km you'll turn right by 'The Keepers Cottage'. About 300m after this, turn left on a signed path along a field edge, taking you down to the Nature Reserve. Follow signs on this rather wet and occasionally indistinct path through the Nature Reserve for about 1km to reach the Lowestoft Road.

E: Turn left on the road for about 700m to the top of the hill, then turn right on a signed footpath. Keep on the right hand side of the hedge, passing Smear Farm in about 700m. Stay on the farm road to reach a narrow road on a corner in another 300m.

F: Turn left at the corner to reach Covert Road in 400m. (Covert Road is the one straight ahead). Go straight on to reach the car park in 300m.

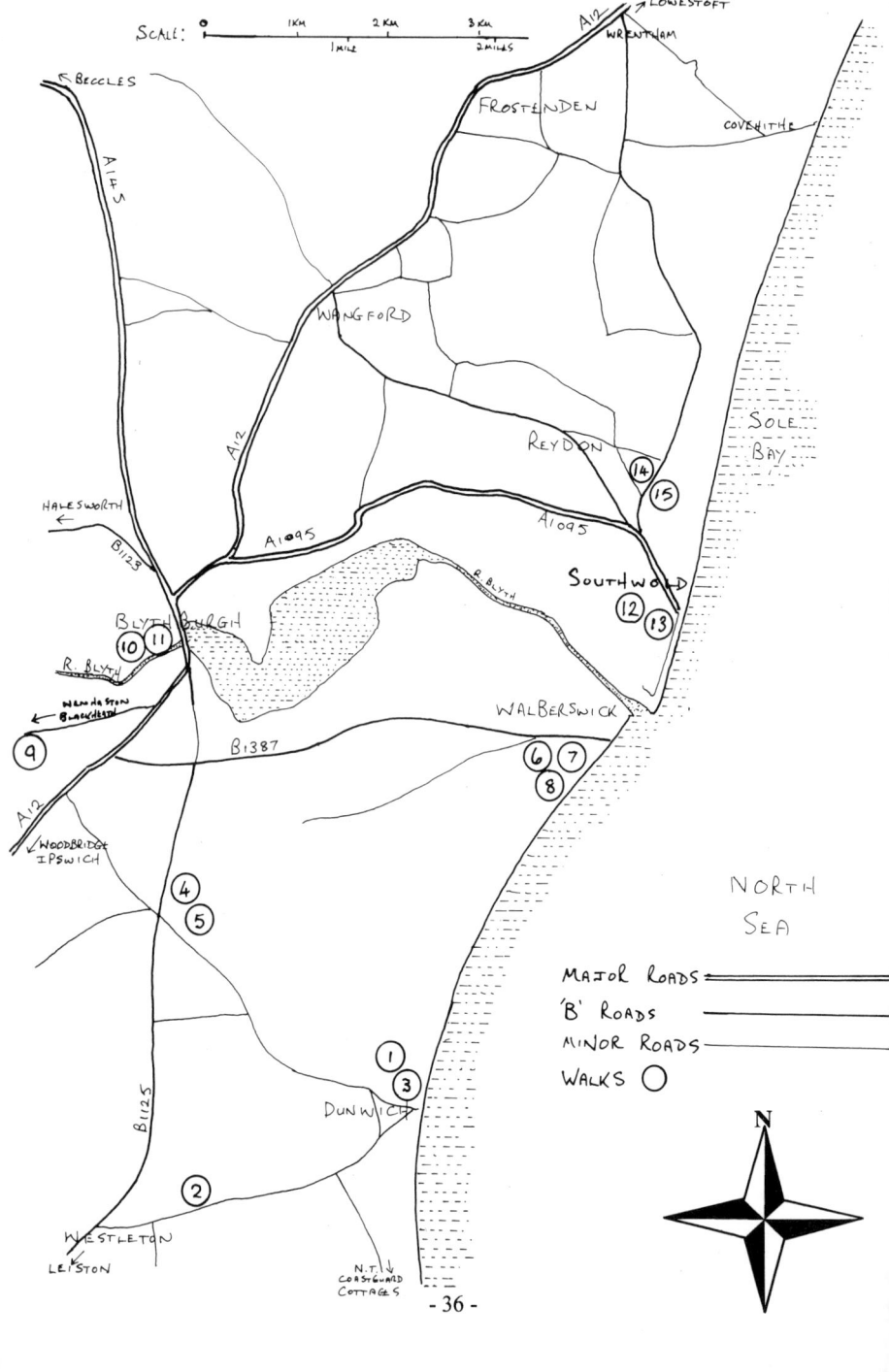